Taliyah
and the Fruit Tree

Written & Illustrated By: Lashami Morrison

Taliyah and the Fruit Tree

Copyright © 2021 Lashami Morrison

Published by:

Relentless Publishing House, LLC

www.relentlesspublishing.com

Printed in USA

ISBN: 978-1-948829694

Acknowledgements

With special thanks:

To my parents, Victor & Joan Morrison and my brother, Victor, Jr., for your unconditional love, support, prayers and always believing in me.

To the love of my life, my fiancé, Jerome Caldwell, Jr., for your love, support, prayers and always being my best friend 🖤

Taliyah
and the Fruit Tree

On one beautiful Saturday afternoon, Taliyah wanted to invite all of her friends over for a sleepover.

."I would love to make something for my friends, but I don't have an idea on what to make," said Taliyah.

"You should go pick some fruit from the tree in the backyard and make some pies," replied mom. "I will be more than happy to help you."

"Here is a list of fruit to pick from the tree," said mom. But there was one problem.

Apple
Cherry
Peach
Strawberry
Blueberry

But there was one problem.

Taliyah did not know how to read! She headed outside to the fruit tree saying to herself, "I must learn how to read this list so I will be able to pick the right fruit for the pies."

"I will help you learn to read," said the fruit tree.
"A talking fruit tree? Wow," said Taliyah. "I would love for you to help me!"

Apple

"Here is the first thing on the list," as Taliyah points to the first word.

"That would be the shiny red fruit to the top left of my branches," said the tree.

Apple

"I have seen that fruit before. That's an APPLE," Taliyah said joyously.

"Good job! The letter 'A' makes the 'ah' sound, like at the beginning of the word 'apple'," said the tree.

Cherry

Peach

"The next two things on the list are the fruits to the top right of my branches," said the tree.

Cherry

Peach

Taliyah grabbed the two fruits and bit into them and replied, "This one tastes just like a peach and the other tastes like a cherry."

"Yes! You're right!" exclaimed the tree. "The beginning of the word CHERRY and the end of the word PEACH makes a specialized sound when you combined letters "c" and "h". It makes the "ch" sound.

Strawberry

Blueberry

"Now, the last two things on the list are on the bottom of my branches," the tree said.

"That's a strawberry! It's my favorite fruit!" Taliyah said excitingly. "But I don't know what the other fruit is."

"You are correct," said the tree. "The other is a blueberry."

"Ohhhh," said Taliyah. "The end of the word blueberry sounds just like the end of the word strawberry."

"You're right," replied the tree. "Making sure you sound out words by their individual letters will help you read!"

"Wow! Thank you so much fruit tree," replied Taliyah. "Now I know when I'm trying to read a word, sounding out each letter will help me." "You're welcome," said the fruit tree. "If you need any more help learning how to read, you know where to find me."

Taliyah headed back in the house with a basket full of the different fruits.

"Mommy, look what I have!" Taliyah said excitingly. "Our fruit tree helped me pick them out and also how to read the list you gave me!"

"Awesome job sweetie," replied mom. "Now we can start making the pies before your friends get here."

Taliyah and her mom started making the different kinds of fruit pies. After two hours went by, the pies were done and her friends had arrived.

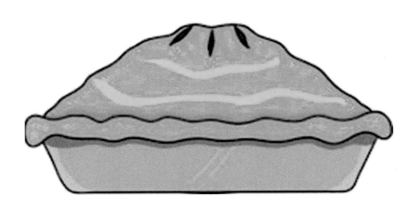

"Hmmmm, something sure does smell good," said one of Taliyah's friends." "I made something I'm sure you will love," replied Taliyah.

"Pies!" said cheerfully by her friends. "Yes, and I learned how to say the different fruits we used to make them," said Taliyah.

Taliyah was very happy about how the pies turned out, but most importantly learned how to read and pronounce the fruits she used.

Taliyah and her friends loved all of the fruit pies and enjoyed the rest of the Saturday afternoon.

The End

About The Author

Lashami Morrison is a fascinating, compelling school teacher who loves to make a difference in children's lives.

She began her studies at Winston Salem State University with a B.A. in Early Childhood Education and continued with her MBA at Strayer University. Lashami began writing in college and dreamed of one day writing a children's book. With her persistence and determination, she prevailed.